Music To My Ears

Bertha Gabriel

BookLeaf Publishing

India | USA | UK

Made with ❤ on the BookLeaf Publishing Platform
www.bookleafpub.in
www.bookleafpub.com

Dedication

To everyone who hears the song behind the poem. Just as ancient King David wrote many Psalms in the Holy Scriptures, I dedicate this book to all those that feel enlightened, inspired and encouraged by melodious words of peace and truth.

Preface

Come to know the different ways to express your inner most thoughts. With fun wordplay and exciting imagery, this book of poems is sure to leave you wanting part 2. Feel hope, comfort, guidance, love. Remanence over good days and find out how to put into words the hurt of lost time. Be inspired and relieved. Come into the melody with me.

Acknowledgements

First off, I can do nothing without the help of my Great God, Jehovah. Also, to everyone who has ever written down words of poetry to express what is in their hearts, you are beautiful.

Nature - Chapter 1.

A Fence Through the Sun

I see the fence through the sun
The sun through the fence
I see the light shining bright
And in my heart relent
I'm up above—up so high
Soaring toward the sky.
I feel the heat, I see the street
My mind cannot beat.
I love the sky; I love the sun.
I love the Creator, One.
I see the sky, I see the fence,
A fence through the sun.

The Sun's Shadow

As I wake up in the morning, I can see the sunlight peeking from the horizon. It's warm intensive feeling moves me to roll over and smile within. I wait for its face to shine right through the window. I lie in wait as it creates the light I'm in. Slowly the sun creeps up and everything begins to wake, it's amazing. I lie in wait for it to break the shadow the sun puts me in. Alive and well, I breathe the light that comes into me. It covers the earth, the sun and its birth, a new day again.

Life - Chapter 2.

Numbers

46 paces till the crowd passes by

51 faces with tears in their eyes.

23 bodies lying cold in the dust.

64 people saying 'fight not! We must!'

33 soldiers marching high as the sky.

99, yet, of them shot down and died.

15 women with bullets in their chest.

4 of them say 'fight on, then go rest'

72 laborers ask to be released.

72 laborers tired of working on their knees.

89 servants left without work.

5 of them call the governor a jerk.

10 wild dogs released to attack.

100 people struggle and fight back

57 say they're living life by getting away.

49 soldiers laugh and say 'ha! This isn't a play!'

94 lives try to get on a ship.

56 lives take a grave watery dip.

38 people see a new world at hand.

3 more although, illness took its stand.

2 people see the statue of liberty

35 souls cry out, "We have been set free!"

16 say new lives for the brave ones.

91 soldiers and look what they've done.

7 children ask, "to live when will we take flight?"

1 person says, "maybe another night."

Before the Night

Before the night
There will be day
Mischief and mystery
On their way
Top to bottom
You'll get what's coming
Never escaping
Unless you're cunning
Move swift and fine
Dodge everything
Find what is divine
And collect your means
Hurry to your spot
A special hiding place
From cold to hot
Day is being replaced
Night's coming soon
To replace the sun
The awakening moon
Two equals one
Portray the darkness
To bloodshed and guilt
The stabbing of sharpness
Die if you will

Hold the burden
Upon your head
Knowing no curtain
That'll cover the dead
Hiding won't do
Because the day is still
They're going to get you
Upon the hill
Before the Night

Return to Day

Return to day
As though it may
Release the strife
That pulls away
Continue strong
Remain alarmed
For what can go wrong
By staying unarmed
Begin to see
Elements of past
Reveal to thee
The gold at last
Your dreams come true
With chance to match
Believing in you
Never let dispatch
All shadows grow cold
All ponds aren't steep
All hearts can't hold
In the watery deep
Mistakes are made
For all do fall
Yet prices repaid
If heeding the call

Temporary flare
May bring no light
The shimmering glare
Will make up for fright
For then be free
As many may
Collected and pleased
Return to Day

Proof is in Memory

Take a photo
Then you'll see
That proof is in your memory
And carefully
Tie down truths
Which in your mind needs no reproof
Remember times
Of long last
That harbors in your moments' past
Which opens up
Crying eyes
That lingers in memory's lies
Yet in the end
Proof is shown
To be what truth has left alone

Turn

To dwell on pain
Is to dwell on sorrow
And to dwell on everything
That'll just come again tomorrow
Let go of anger
And push back rage
Leave presumptuousness alone
Keep abuse in its cage
Conquer evil
Of course with good
And leave anxiety for tomorrow
Remaining where it should
Deal with now
Not letting the sun set
Because to give way to violence
Just fills one with regret

Reasonable Enough

Not enough cash, not enough time
But just enough to make you mine
Not a big house and not a nice car
Though it takes me places near or far
Not the right clothing; not the right tie
Yet the right amount of clothes to fit my size
Not all the glamour of those who are rich
Sweet, kind or maybe even tough
But this life is reasonable enough

A Broken Man

What is a man unbroken?
First what is a broken man?
One who sobs all over, all across in many lands.
One who sits on stools behind the bar counter.
One who isn't afraid but wouldn't be a big announcer.
A man lied to, misguided and cheated out of everything.
But what is the opposite of this, what does it mean?
Displeasure isn't inside him and shame may play within.
But he is the happiest person, because with the truth he
does live.
A man broken has lost the love that was once in his
heart.
And he's a pity to look upon, because something tore it
apart.
What is a broken man?
Yet what is a man unbroken?
Love and cherish, respect him; and don't be hasty to
doubt.
If such actions are taken, good things it'll bring about.
Remember though that when times get rough, to rebuild
a broken man will be pretty tough.

Not Faultless

13

Do not stand there a hypocrite!
Hypocrite!
Do not speak!
Do not give me guidelines!
Guidelines!
You won't keep!
Do not say, "Do as I say!"
As I say!
"And not as I do!"
Do not stand there a hypocrite!
Hypocrite!
I am too.

We Drink Brandy

Sitting around the table, looking outside
We sigh…another day's gone.
How happy we are to be with friends.
Love, laughter added to memory books.
Relating experiences from the day.
How nice it is to be relaxed.
At peace, we keep on looking out.
We watch as the birds fly over the water.
Peaceful; so we grab a glass.
Ah! Brandy! Let us drink.
Warms the stomach, warms the mouth
Soothes the heart. A gift from God.
We quietly sit after our sip. (Sip)
Mm. "Good stuff." Good night.

Death - Chapter 3.

Relentless

Before the night is over
Before the day is done
Within the counter's border
You'll see an iron tong.
Put all the food in order
And erect the bold white sign
Stand shoulder to shoulder
And place the chairs in line.
All in black attire
Dressed for the dead
Everything is down to the wire
With walls of ruby red.
In a methodized manner
All reactions fully shown
Headed down the rusty ladder
Into the catacomb
Laying one to rest
And walking back to light
Before the sun sets

Everything is done right
Now for the feast
And time to go on
And for once all released
What was never gone.

We Follow the Dead

We follow the dead
Yes, to the cemetery
Line as long as a train
With cars following the fallen
Black attire or dark dress
We all follow to lay one to rest
Such a sad time it is
To be traveling on a day
Knowing that at the front
Was someone special
Yet death catches us all
For it is truly a disease - genetic
A menacing pirate
That takes one's life in a moment
Looking out the window
While sitting in the car
Watching as the rest of the world
Continues on in life
It makes one wonder
When death will end
But for now, it's still here
And we still follow the dead

Faith - Chapter 4.

The Final Condition

The hour is coming
When we'll soon celebrate
The ending of evil
Which none can escape
With thought of a resurrection
And a hope for the dead
Soon no one will cry
Over too much bloodshed
So should I be worried
When these things are to be?
No, I have no fright
You see no shiver in me
Yet some may not realize
All prophesied in Revelation
But soon God will destroy
All wicked men in the nations
Away Satan will be
No longer in his position

And this my friends
Is the final condition

The Checkered Cell (Part 1)

"Come sit with me, my loving friend
Be in the peace that I'm in
Be worry free, though full of sin
And come sit with me, my loving friend."

He said these words as he looked afar
Behind closed doors, behind checkered bars
Within the hollow cell that leaked
You'd hear him sigh, and then he'd speak...

"Come sit with me, my loving friend
Be in the peace that I'm in
Be worry free, though full of sin-
And come sit with me, my loving friend."

To whom was he referring?
One may never know
To whom was he speaking?
To us...here below?
Within himself he'll be in peace
And that talking will never cease
But at that moment, as he looks through the bars
He's full of remorse and battered with scars.

O man inside, as you sit, be well
Sing us a song within your checkered cell...

Pure Majesty

O my Great and Grand Jehovah
Whom over all rules everything
You set all things in motion
Joy and happiness you bring
How I love you, O my Sovereign
How I see no better course
Than to give myself to you
The One through which life finds its source
I want to serve forever and ever
I want to do all things good
I want to be your daughter someday
When everything is as it should
I love you, O my Sovereign
You do all things so chaste
You cleanse out all wickedness
Even sin doesn't have a place
I love your Grand Creation
By which you truly speak
I marvel at your beauty
Far beyond the mountain peek
I wonder O Jehovah,
How it all was made to be
It's so wonderful your Creation
I'm so happy that I can see!

You deserve the praise
The honor, wisdom, love- all things
You are Great, O Grand Jehovah
You are Pure Majesty!

Love - Chapter 5.

My Heart's Choir

Race with me
If you please
Then leave me
You can go
Comfort me
In the light
Oh darkness
Coming night
Don't linger here
Then disappear
When you're needed most
My heart and mind
Must thus decline
If this is how you boast
Race in me
O bleeding heart
And waver
Never please
When coming dark

Is close in part
To these atrocities
Rescue me
O dying light
From darkness' trickery
And shelter me
If you please
From myself
The one who pleas

Kiss Me Goodnight

May sweetness grow
As tender loves do
And may feelings show
What others show too
When darkness falls
And night reaches it height
Your name I will call
To kiss me goodnight
Beside you I shall lay
And together we'll rise
If with passion I should pay
Your love I will not despise
Come to me whole
With heart and mind
Rest with my frail soul
And let our words remain kind
Upon me lies his gentle hand
He kisses me goodnight, this loving man.

Where the Heart Does Not Belong

Emotions are in line
For things that are too strong
And impatience only leads
To where the heart does not belong
Recline on silk and lust
On riches, silver, gold...
Reach high up toward the sky
Until the day gets old
Yet something never changes
When such things do take place
It's the destructive end
In the heart's own desperate pace.
Why cower under pressure?
Pressure that leads to dust
Why not do all things that are pleasing?
Pleasing, right and just
Let mind control the matter
Within the chest that beats
Because with a pure conscience
Bad habits will not repeat.
So conquer, yes conquer
Things that the heart does wrong

And keep that heart from going
To where the heart does not belong

Fiction - Chapter 6.

Ragina on Her Throne

Ragina, Ragina on her throne, sitting there lonely, cold, and alone. Mighty she seems in appearance at glare. Challenge her no one ever does dare. Yet who knows Ragina on her throne? When truthfully, she does sit there cold and alone? Decorated with rags that she has. Never one leaving her sight nor will she let it pass. Red hair bright as blood and eyes dark as night. She smiles all the time, so she is a true fright. But really as she sits with a tear in her heart, will anyone have any care on her part? As lovely as she may seem, into the blank air she always beams. Her nose is red and so are her lips. She has no thighs and she has no hips. O woe for Ragina! What will she do? Soon the time will draw near and she has no clue. With red and white stockings she is attached. So on the day of despoil, she'll surely dispatch. But wait and see, she's still there sitting down. Having no tears, no, not a single frown. Surely, she wears the crown for today. Maybe more, even each day. Yet one thing I know, she's the best at what she does too. She sits there and stare and reads, "I love you". Can words be simpler to say out loud? To wash away victory with the clouds? No, away she likes to be alone. Ragina, Ragina, on her throne.

L and R

Long before the time is breached

Underscore the lying sheets

Releasing winds that are of strength

And never leaves of complaint

Through the open door do go

Flying high as arrow's bow

Refreshing times of summer breeze

And going by each day with ease

Lovely, though, let play the song

Melodious tunes and sing along

Return to trees of gentle glow

And to me let true feelings show

Complain if the sun is, oh too bright

But do not wait for darkness of night

Repeat the trend until the end

And once completed, begin again.